My First French Picture Dictionary

Illustrated by Nick Sharratt

Written by Christine Mabileau and Irene Yates

Consultant Editors Natasha Farrant and Ginny Lapage

PARROT

First edition for the United States and Canada published by
Barron's Educational Series, Inc., in 2001.

Published by arrangement with HarperCollins*Publishers* Ltd

First published in 2001 by HarperCollins*Children's Books*,
a division of HarperCollins*Publishers* Ltd

Text and illustrations copyright © 2001 by HarperColllins*Publishers* Ltd

All inquiries should be addressed to:
Barron's Educational Series, Inc.
250 Wireless Boulevard
Hauppauge, New York 11788
http://www.barronseduc.com

International Standard Book No. 0-7641-5436-2
Library of Congress Catalog Card No. 2001087558

Printed in Hong Kong
9 8 7 6 5 4 3 2 1

Contents

How to use this book

Tom

Elisha

Jake

Children love playing with words, and learning a new language can be lots of fun. This colorful dictionary is specially designed to help you introduce your child to French. With your help, your child will learn key words from a range of familiar situations, discovering new sounds along the way. They will also start to recognize some of the differences and similarities between French and English.

First steps to learning French

As soon as they are comfortable expressing themselves in their own language, children are ready to learn a new one. To get the most out of this book, sit with your child and encourage them to look at the pictures, to say the French words as often as possible,

Read the heading out loud so your child knows the context of the French words.

Point to the picture, then run your finger along the French words, from left to right, saying the words out loud. Ask you child to repeat the words, not forgetting to say the short word in front.

Compare the French word with the English, pointing out the similarities as well as the differences between the two languages.

Look for me on every page – sometimes you will have to look very hard! It's fun to see what I'm doing.

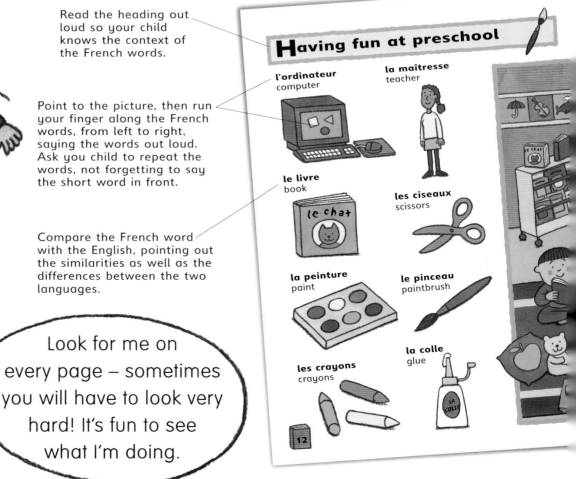

Having fun at preschool

l'ordinateur
computer

la maîtresse
teacher

le livre
book

les ciseaux
scissors

la peinture
paint

le pinceau
paintbrush

les crayons
crayons

la colle
glue

12

and to answer all the questions. Come back to the book time and time again, so your child absorbs the new sounds and learns to associate the French words with the pictures.

Questions and answers

Nick Sharrat's lively scenes will help your child to memorize the French words by putting them into context. They also offer plenty of scope for further questions, so you can encourage your child to practice speaking their newly learned words. For your own guidance, there is a pronunciation guide at the back of the book.

Lucy

Taz

Amy

Ask the questions, encouraging your child always to answer in French. (The answers will be words featured on the spread.)

Food to help me grow

What's white and good to drink?

le fromage
cheese

les fruits
fruit

les œufs
eggs

les légumes
vegetables

le riz
rice

le hamburger
hamburger

le poisson
fish

le poulet
chicken

les biscuits
cookies

la pizza
pizza

le pain
bread

le yaourt
yogurt

27

What do you use to cut things up?

Encourage your child to point out and name real objects around them whenever possible.

Make up your own questions, based on what's going on in the picture. Once your child has learned about colors and numbers (see pages 40–43), you can incorporate these in your questions too, for example, "How many paintbrushes can you count?"

Learning the names of the characters will add to the fun your child gets from using this book.

What is the little boy reading?

Ask your child to match objects in the main picture with those shown on the left, and vice versa. When looking for an object, encourage your child always to use its French name.

5

Fun and games at home

la porte
door

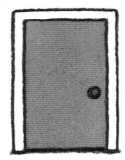

la fenêtre
window

la chaise
chair

le canapé
sofa

le coussin
cushion

la pendule
clock

la télévision
television

le téléphone
telephone

Look at me!

la tête
head

les cheveux
hair

le visage
face

le nez
nose

les yeux
eyes

les oreilles
ears

les dent
teeth

la bouche
mouth

le cou
neck

l'épaule
shoulder

What do you smell things with?

8

Come to my birthday party

le ballon
balloon

le masque
mask

le cadeau
present

le chapeau en papier
party hat

la glace
ice cream

le gâteau
cake

le jus de fruit
fruit juice

les bonbons
candies

10

Having fun at preschool

l'ordinateur
computer

la maîtresse
teacher

le livre
book

le chat

les ciseaux
scissors

la peinture
paint

le pinceau
paintbrush

la colle
glue

les crayons
crayons

LA COLLE

12

la veste
jacket

la chemise
shirt

le pantalon
pants

la jupe
skirt

la robe
dress

le short
shorts

les chaussettes
socks

les chaussures
shoes

What do you like to wear best?

14

Let's play in the yard

la tondeuse
lawnmower

la brouette
wheelbarrow

le papillon
butterfly

l'oiseau
bird

l'arrosoir
watering pail

le vélo
bike

la pataugeoire
kiddie pool

la fleur
flower

Take a walk down our street

la maison
house

le magasin
shop

l'agent de police
policeman

la route
road

la voiture
car

le lampadaire
street light

le fauteuil roulant
wheelchair

les feux
traffic light

Where do you go to buy things?

18

Things that go

les rollers
rollerblades

le camion
truck

le bus
bus

la moto
motorbike

l'excavateur
backhoe

le camion benne
dump truck

le bateau
ship

le skateboard
skateboard

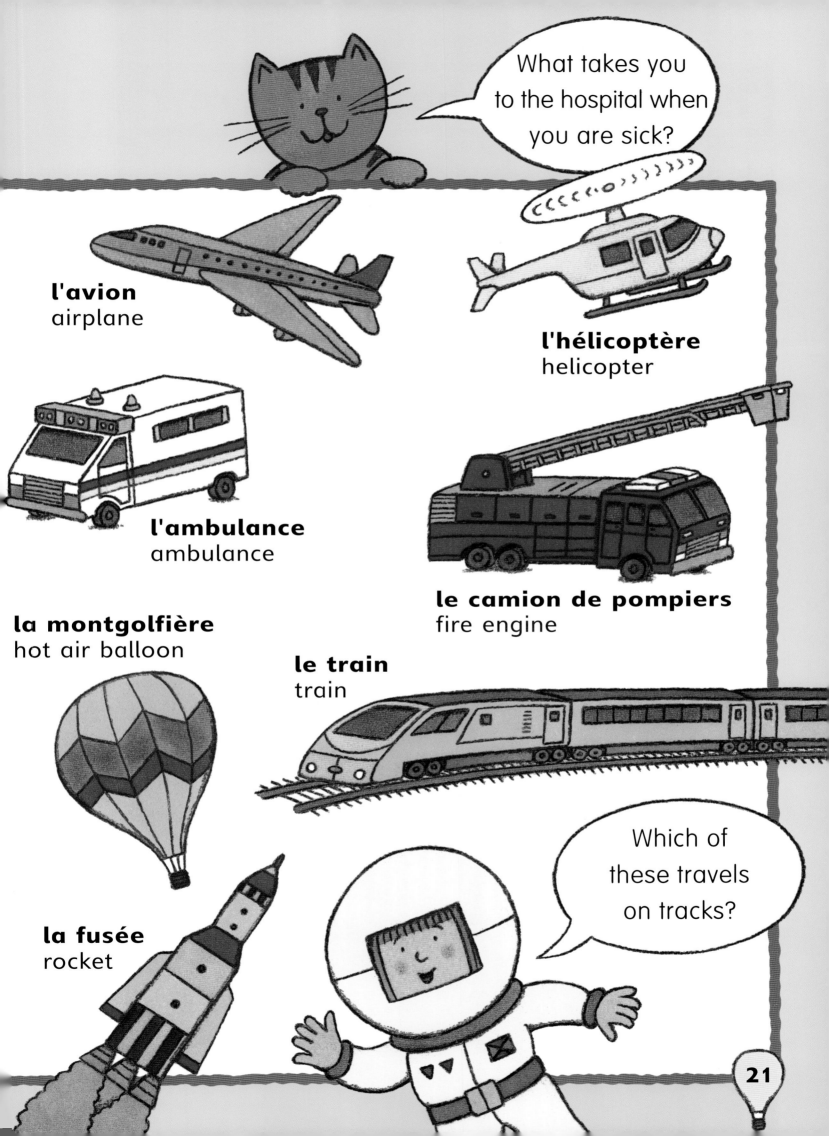

l'avion
airplane

l'hélicoptère
helicopter

l'ambulance
ambulance

le camion de pompiers
fire engine

la montgolfière
hot air balloon

le train
train

la fusée
rocket

What takes you to the hospital when you are sick?

Which of these travels on tracks?

Let's go to the toy store

le puzzle
jigsaw puzzle

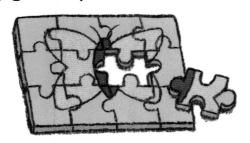

le camion
truck

le garage
garage

la maison de poupées
dollhouse

l'ours en peluche
teddy bear

la poupée
doll

la marionnette
puppet

les cubes
blocks

22

At the supermarket

le bocal
jar

le sac
bag

la boîte de conserve
can

le panier
basket

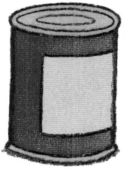

le caddy
shopping cart

l'argent
money

la caisse
checkout counter

la bouteille
bottle

Food to help me grow

les fruits
fruit

les légumes
vegetables

le riz
rice

le hamburger
hamburger

les frites
French fries

les spaghetti
spaghetti

les céréales
cereal

What do you eat for breakfast?

26

Take me to the pet store

le lapin
rabbit

le hamster
hamster

le chaton
kitten

le chiot
puppy

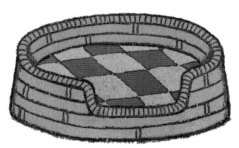

le poisson rouge
goldfish

le panier
basket

la cage
cage

la perruche
parakeet

What's in the park?

le toboggan
slide

la balançoire
swing

la poussette
stroller

la cage à grimper
jungle gym

le banc
bench

l'arbre
tree

le chien
dog

le canard
duck

30

Big beasts and minibeasts

le kangourou
kangaroo

le lion
lion

la girafe
giraffe

le panda
panda

l'éléphant
elephant

le crocodile
crocodile

la baleine
whale

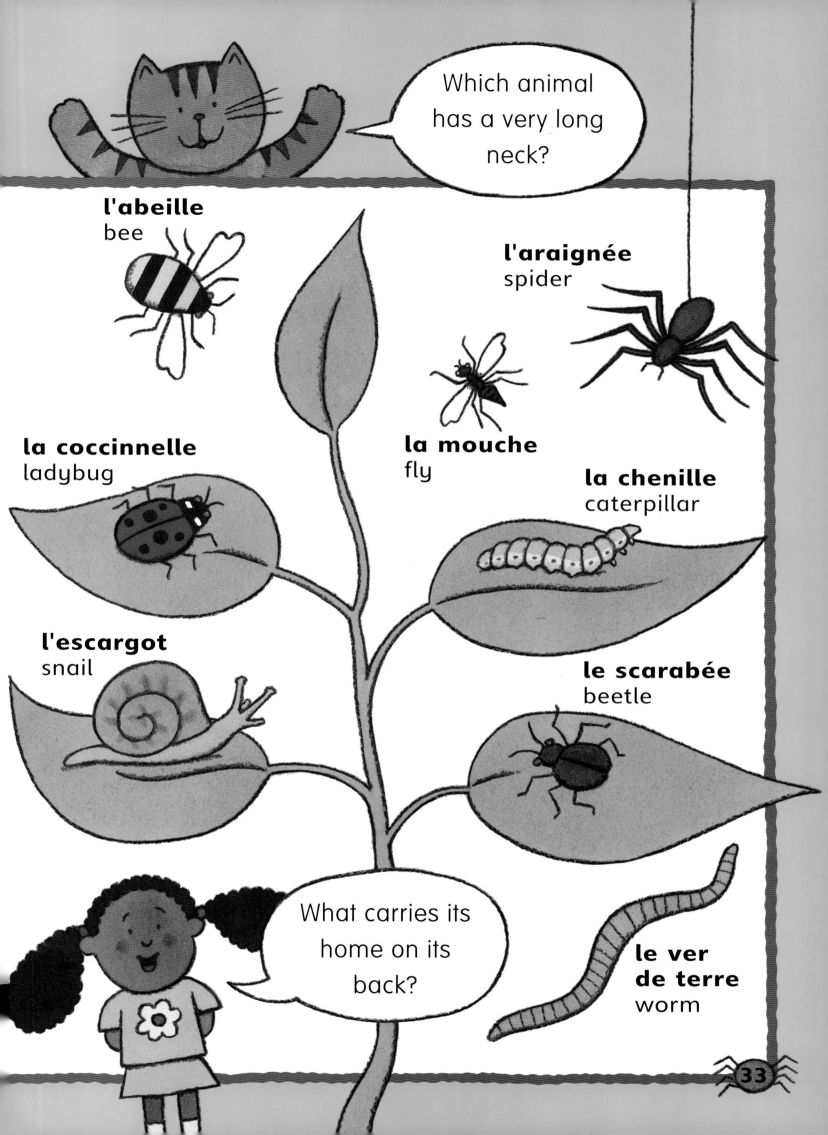

Down on the farm

le fermier
farmer

le tracteur
tractor

la poule
hen

l'agneau
lamb

le cheval
horse

la vache
cow

la barrière
gate

le foin
hay

34

A sunny day at the seashore

le coquillage
shell

le crabe
crab

la mouette
seagull

le château de sable
sand castle

le ballon de plage
beach ball

la vague
wave

le seau
pail

la pelle
shovel

See what we can do!

il saute
he jumps

il marche
he walks

elle court
she runs

elle applaudit
she claps

elle porte
she carries

What is the girl with the box doing?

il peint
he paints

ils dansent they dance

38

Colors are everywhere

violet
purple

rouge
red

noir
black

bleu
blue

jaune
yellow

What color is the bouncy castle?

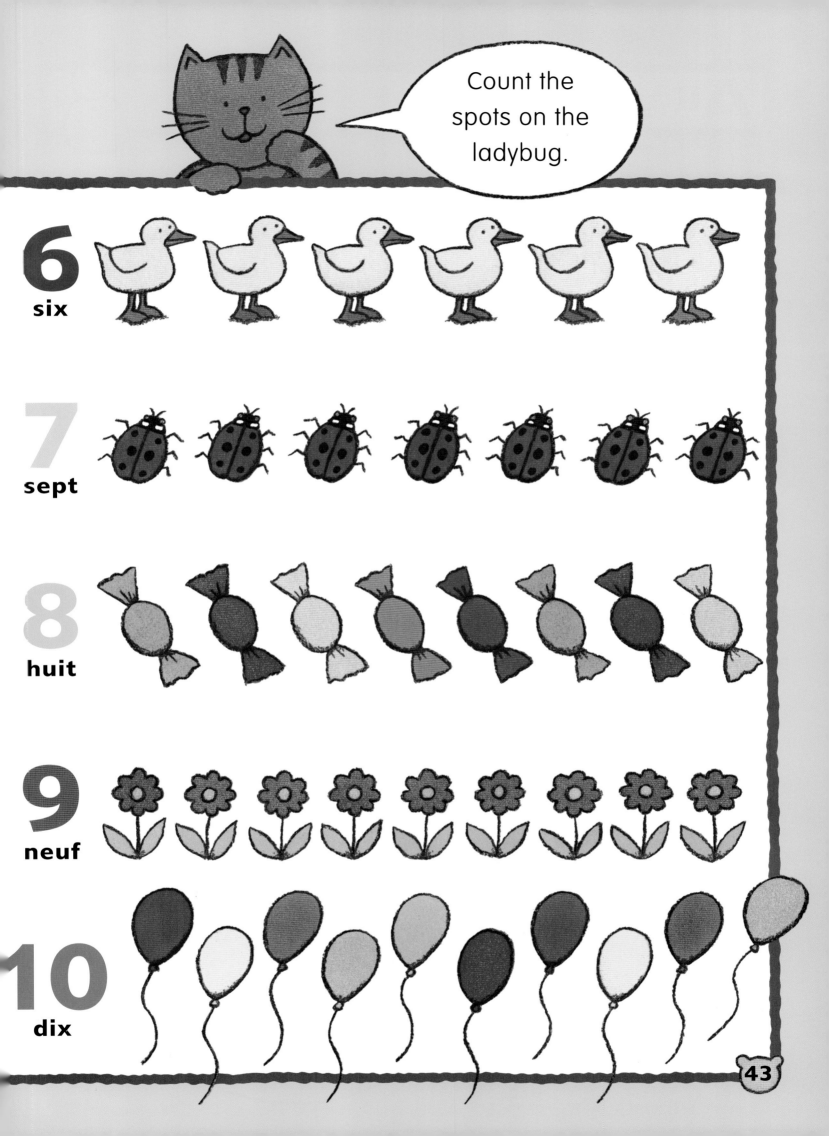

6 six

7 sept

8 huit

9 neuf

10 dix

43

All year round

lundi
Monday

mardi
Tuesday

mercredi
Wednesday

jeudi
Thursday

vendredi
Friday

samedi
Saturday

dimanche
Sunday

le jour
day

la nuit
night

What day of the week is it?

What makes you put up your umbrella?

le soleil
sun

la pluie
rain

le vent
wind

la neige
snow

How the words sound

A guide to pronunciation

French pronunciation is different from English, and some French sounds do not exist in English. Pronunciations are shown in italics, with some of the main differences highlighted in bold as follows:

an is close to ph**o**ne as in "mange" – m**an**j
e is close to el**e**vator as in "le"– **le** and "deux" – d**e**
in is close to s**ang** as in "lapin" – lap**in**
j is close to plea**su**re as in "genou" – **j**enoo
on is close to so**ng** as in "bonbon" – b**on**b**on**
u is close to L**u**ke as in "pendule" –p**an**d**u**l

French nouns are masculine or feminine and should be learned with "le" or "la" in front of them. "Les" is used for plural.

A

airplane	l'avion – lavy**on**
ambulance	l'ambulance – l**an**bul**an**s
arm	le bras – **le** bra

B

backhoe	l'excavateur – lexkavat**e**r
bag	le sac – **le** sak
balloon	le ballon – **le** bal**on**
basket	le panier – **le** panyay
beach ball	le ballon de plage –
	le bal**on** d**e** pla**j**
bee	l'abeille – labay
beetle	le scarabée – **le** scarabay
bench	le banc – **le** b**an**
bike	le vélo – **le** vaylo
bird	l'oiseau – lwazo
black	noir – nwar
blocks	les cubes – lay k**u**b
blue	bleu – bl**e**
book	le livre – **le** leevr
bottle	la bouteille – la bootay
bottom	le derrière – **le** deryayr
boxers	le caleçon – **le** kals**on**
bread	le pain – **le** p**an**
brown	marron – mar**on**
brushes, she	elle brosse – el bros

| bus | le bus – **le** b**u**s |
| butterfly | le papillon – **le** papeey**on** |

C

cage	la cage – la ka**j**
cake	le gâteau – **le** gato
can	la boîte de conserve –
	la bwat d**e** k**on**serv
car	la voiture – la vwat**u**r
carries, she	elle porte – el port
caterpillar	la chenille – la sheneey
cereal	les céréales – lay sayrayhal
chair	la chaise – la shez
checkout counter	la caisse – la kess
cheese	le fromage – **le** froma**j**
chicken	le poulet – **le** poolay
claps, she	elle applaudit – el aplodee
clock	la pendule – la p**an**d**u**l
computer	l'ordinateur – lordinat**e**r
cookies	les biscuits – lay beeskwee
cow	la vache – la vash
crab	le crabe – **le** krab
cries, he	il pleure – eel pl**e**r
crocodile	le crocodile – **le** krokodeel
cushion	le coussin – **le** koos**sin**
cuts, she	elle coupe – el koop

D

dance, they	ils dansent – eel d**an**s
day	le jour – **le** joor
dog	le chien – **le** shee**in**
doll	la poupée – la poopay
dollhouse	la maison de poupées –
	la mayz**on** d**e** poopay
door	la porte – la port
dress	la robe – la rob
drinks, she	elle boit – el bwa
duck	le canard – **le** kanar
dump truck	le camion benne –
	le kamy**on** ben

E

ears	les oreilles – lay zoray
eats, she	elle mange – el m**an**j
eggs	les œufs – lay z**e**
eight	huit – weet

46

elbow	le coude – *le kood*		**K**	
elephant	l'éléphant – *lelefan*		kangaroo	le kangourou – *le kangooroo*
eyes	les yeux – *layzye*		kiddie pool	la pataugeoire – *la patojwar*
			kitten	le chaton – *le shaton*
F			knee	le genou – *le jenoo*
face	le visage – *le veezaj*			
farmer	le fermier – *le fayrmyay*		**L**	
finger	le doigt – *le dwa*		ladybug	la coccinnelle – *la cokseenel*
fire engine	le camion de pompiers –		lamb	l'agneau – *lanyo*
	le kamyon de ponpyay		laughs, he	il rit – *eel ree*
fish	le poisson – *le pwasson*		lawnmower	la tondeuse – *la tonderz*
five	cinq – *sink*		leg	la jambe – *la janb*
flower	la fleur – *la fler*		lion	le lion – *le lyon*
fly	la mouche – *la moosh*			
foot	le pied – *le pyay*		**M**	
four	quatre – *katr*		mask	le masque – *le mask*
French fries	les frites – *lay freet*		milk	le lait – *le lay*
Friday	vendredi – *vandredee*		Monday	lundi – *landee*
fruit	les fruits – *lay frwee*		money	l'argent – *larjan*
fruit juice	le jus de fruit – *le ju de frwee*		motor bike	la moto – *la moto*
			mouth	la bouche – *la bush*
G				
garage	le garage – *le garaj*		**N**	
gate	la barrière – *la baryayr*		night	la nuit – *la nwee*
giraffe	la girafe – *la jeeraf*		nightgown	la chemise de nuit –
gloves	les gants – *lay gan*			*la shemeez de nwee*
glue	la colle – *la kol*		nine	neuf – *nerf*
goldfish	le poisson rouge – *le pwasson rooj*		nose	le nez – *le nay*
green	vert – *vayr*		neck	le cou – *le koo*
H			**O**	
hair	les cheveux – *lay sheve*		one	un – *an*
hamburger	le hamburger – *le hamburger*		orange	orange – *oranj*
hamster	le hamster – *le amster*			
hand	la main – *la min*		**P**	
hat	le bonnet – *le bonay*		pail	le seau – *le so*
hay	le foin – *le fwin*		paints, he	il peint – *eel pin*
head	la tête – *la tet*		paintbrush	le pinceau – *le pinso*
helicopter	l'hélicoptère – *lelikoptayr*		pajamas	le pyjama – *le peejama*
hen	la poule – *la pool*			
horse	le cheval – *le sheval*			
hot air balloon	la montgolfière – *la mongolfyear*			
house	la maison – *la mayzon*			
I J				
ice cream	la glace – *la glass*			
jacket	la veste – *la vest*			
jar	le bocal – *le bokal*			
jigsaw puzzle	le puzzle – *le puzl*			
jumps, he	il saute – *eel sot*			
jungle gym	la cage à grimper –			
	la kaj a grinpay			

panda	le panda – *le panda*		spaghetti	les spaghetti – *lay spaghetti*
panties	la culotte – *la kulot*		spider	l'araignée – *laraynyay*
pants	le pantalon – *le pantalon*		street light	le lampadaire – *le lanpadayr*
parakeet	la peruche – *la perush*		stroller	la poussette – *la poosset*
party hat	le chapeau en papier –		sun	le soleil – *le solay*
	le shapo an papyay		Sunday	dimanche – *deemansh*
pen	les crayons – *lay krayon*		sweater	le pull – *le pul*
pink	rose – *rose*		sweets	les bonbons – *lay bonbon*
pizza	la pizza – *la peedza*		swing	la balançoire – *la balanswar*
policeman	l'agent de police – *lajan de police*			
present	le cadeau – *le kado*		**T**	
puppet	la marionnette – *la maryonet*			
puppy	le chiot – *le shyo*		teacher	la maîtresse – *la maytrayss*
purple	violet – *vyolay*		teddy bear	l'ours en peluche – *loors an pelush*
			teeth	les dents – *lay dan*
R			telephone	le téléphone – *le telefon*
			television	la télévision – *la televeezyon*
rabbit	le lapin – *le lapin*		ten	dix – *deess*
rain	la pluie – *la plwee*		three	trois – *trwa*
red	rouge – *rooj*		thumb	le pouce – *le pooss*
rice	le riz – *le ree*		Thursday	jeudi – *jedee*
road	la route – *la root*		toe	l'orteil – *lortay*
rocket	la fusée – *la fuzay*		tractor	le tracteur – *le trakter*
rollerblades	les rollers – *lay roller*		traffic light	les feux – *lay fe*
runs, she	elle court – *el koor*		train	le train – *le trin*
			tree	l'arbre – *larbr*
S			truck	le camion – *le kamyon*
			T-shirt	le T-shirt – *le tee-shirt*
sand castle	le château de sable –		Tuesday	mardi – *mardee*
	le shato de sable		tummy	le ventre – *le vantr*
Saturday	samedi – *samedee*		two	deux – *de*
scissors	les ciseaux – *lay seezo*			
seagull	la mouette – *la mwet*		**U V W**	
seven	sept – *set*			
shell	le coquillage – *le kokeeyaj*		vegetables	les légumes – *lay laygum*
ship	le bateau – *le bato*		walks, he	il marche – eel *marsh*
shirt	la chemise – *la shemeez*		watering pail	l'arrosoir – *larozwar*
shoes	les chaussures – *lay shossur*		wave	la vague – *la vague*
shop	le magasin – *le magazin*		Wednesday	mercredi – *mayrcredee*
shopping cart	le caddy – *le kadee*		whale	la baleine – *la balen*
shorts	le short – *le short*		wheelbarrow	la brouette – *la broohet*
shoulder	l'épaule – *laypol*		wheelchair	le fauteuil roulant – *le fotey roolan*
shovel	la pelle – *la pel*		white	blanc – *blan*
sings, he	il chante – eel *shant*		wind	le vent – *le van*
six	six – *seess*		window	la fenêtre – *la fenetr*
skateboard	le skateboard – *le skateboard*		worm	le ver de terre – *le vayr de tayr*
skirt	la jupe – *la jup*			
slide	le toboggan – *le tobogan*		**X Y Z**	
snail	l'escargot – *leskargo*			
snow	la neige – *la nej*		yellow	jaune – *jon*
socks	les chaussettes – *lay shosset*		yogurt	le yaourt – *le yahoort*
sofa	le canapé – *le kanapay*